The Civil Rights Movement in America

CORNERSTONES
OF FREEDOM™

SECOND SERIES

Elaine Landau

Children's Press®
A Division of Scholastic Inc.
New York • Toronto • London • Auckland • Sydney
Mexico City • New Delhi • Hong Kong
Danbury, Connecticut

Photographs ©2003: AP/Wide World Photos: 26, 33, 40, 45 bottom left;
Brown Brothers: 4; Corbis Images: 14, 15, 16, 18, 23, 39, 44 top right, 45
top (Bettmann), 8 (H.R. Farr), 7; Folio, Inc.: 12, 21 right, 25, 31, 44 top
left, 44 bottom, 44 center; Getty Images: 28 (Birmingham News/Liaison),
35 (Russell Lee); Hulton|Archive/Getty Images 5, 6, 10, 22, 34, 37, 38
bottom, 45 bottom right; Magnum Photos/Bob Adelman: 41 top; Peter
Arnold Inc./James H. Karales: cover top; Photri Inc./Larry Stevens: 3, 32;
Stock Montage, Inc.: cover bottom, 21 left; Stockphoto.com: 29, 30
(Charles Moore), 36 (Steve Schapiro); Woodfin Camp & Associates:
38 top (Bob Adelman), 41 bottom (Dan Budnik).

Library of Congress Cataloging-in-Publication Data
Landau, Elaine.
  The civil rights movement in America / Elaine Landau.
    p. cm. — (Cornerstones of freedom. Second series)
Summary: Relates the history of race relations in the United States,
focusing on the civil rights movement that began in 1954 with the
Supreme Court ruling against segregation in public schools.
  Includes bibliographical references and index.
    ISBN 0-516-24219-9
    1. African Americans—Civil rights—History—20th century—
Juvenile literature. 2. Civil rights movements—History—20th century—
Juvenile literature. 3. United States—Race relations—Juvenile literature.
[1. African Americans—Civil rights—History—20th century. 2. Civil
rights movements—History—20th century. 3. Race relations.] I. Title. II.
Series: Cornerstones of freedom. Second series.
E185.61.L29 2003
323'.0973—dc21

                                                      2003005601

CHILDREN'S PRESS, and CORNERSTONES OF FREEDOM™, and
associated logos are trademarks and or registered trademarks of Scholastic
Library Publishing. SCHOLASTIC and associated logos are trademarks
and or registered trademarks of Scholastic Inc.

1 2 3 4 5 6 7 8 9 10 R 12 11 10 09 08 07 06 05 04 03

I N 1946, A BLACK WORLD War II veteran was traveling by bus home to North Carolina. At a rest stop, the bus driver thought the passenger took too long to return to the bus, so he called the police. The soldier, whose three years in the U.S. Army during World War II included 15 months of active combat duty, was then severely beaten by the police and left blind.

Members of the Ku Klux Klan (KKK) hold a rally in Wrightsville, Georgia, in the 1940s. The activities of white supremacist organizations such as the Klan increased in the years following World War II, as African Americans grew more determined to claim their full civil rights.

This was not unusual punishment for a "mistake" made by an African American at this time in the United States. In fact, some people would have even said he got off lightly. Though slavery had long since been abolished, following the Union's victory in the Civil War, African Americans still had a long, bloody journey ahead to secure equal rights.

White domination of African Americans had long been maintained by both law and violent practice, calling for the occasional example to be made of the black man, woman, or child who "stepped out of line." This ensured that the rest of their community would "know their place" as second-class citizens.

However, events were inspiring new **challenges** to such injustices. On April 11, 1945, for example, an all-black regiment of American soldiers was among the first to arrive at Buchenwald concentration camp in Germany and liberate its survivors from the Nazis. Though they were fighting in Europe to free the victims of the brutally racist Nazi regime of Adolf Hitler, the armed forces in which these soldiers served were still segregated. Having

African Americans who served their country in the military in World War II were made to do so in segregated units. The men in this photograph were members of the famous Tuskegee Airmen, as black Americans trained as military pilots at the Tuskegee Institute in Alabama became known.

★ ★ ★ ★

witnessed firsthand the grotesque consequences of organized racism in Europe, where the Nazis had murdered 6 million Jews, many of these young African-American men were less willing to accept injustice when they returned home.

Two years later in 1947, Jackie Robinson integrated the national pastime when, as a member of the Brooklyn Dodgers, he became the first African American to play major-league baseball. Robinson became a highly visible symbol of the way that the relationship between whites and blacks in American society was changing.

A whipping post was just one of the tools plantation owners in the South used to maintain the system of slavery on which their wealth and prestige depended.

AFRICANS IN AMERICA

In 1619, the first African slaves arrived at the Virginia colony of Jamestown, brought in chains to work the colony's tobacco crop. Over the years, as tobacco and other crops became vital for the economy of the colonies, the institution of slavery was legalized.

Although slavery existed throughout the New World, only in what was to become the United States were all slaves Africans, and almost all Africans slaves. This certainly encouraged the belief, among white Americans, that black Africans were inferior to them. The idea of white supremacy grew stronger as white slave owners sought to justify enslavement and to train the ideal slave to become absolutely dependent on

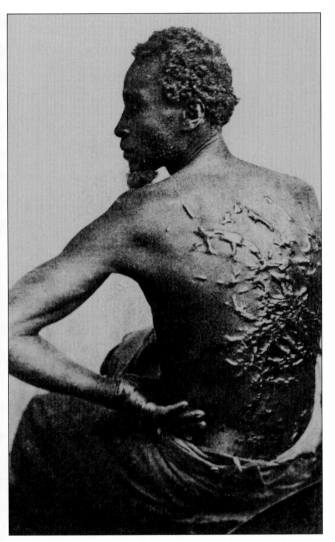

The tracks crisscrossing the back of this former slave, who was photographed during the Civil War, are the scars left by whippings administered by his white owners. Segregation, like slavery, was maintained by the threat and use of violence by whites against blacks.

★ ★ ★ ★

THREE-FIFTHS OF A PERSON

After the Revolutionary War, delegates from the northern and southern states argued about how to count slaves into a state's population. The larger a state's population, the more seats in Congress it could have. Black slaves made up a huge part of the population in southern states but were not allowed to vote. Finally, a compromise was spelled out in Section 2 of Article I in the U.S. Constitution of 1787: slaves would count as "three-fifths" of a person for purposes of taxation and representation.

him. Africans were made to forget and even despise the history and culture of their **ancestors**, while European armed conquests in Africa and elsewhere were cited as proof that whites were superior.

★ ★ ★ ★

Lynching was not only a southern phenomenon, nor the activity of isolated malcontents. This grim photograph shows the lynching of a black man in Minneapolis, Minnesota, in 1882, attended by a large white crowd. Lynchings often brought out a large part of the white community, and postcards made from photos of such events were relatively commonplace in the first part of the 20th century.

THE BLACK EXPERIENCE IN THE RECONSTRUCTION SOUTH

After the Civil War, the Thirteenth Amendment, ratified in 1865, abolished slavery. The Fourteenth Amendment of 1868 gave freed slaves legal rights, and the Fifteenth Amendment of 1870 gave them the right to vote. During the Reconstruction Era, it became obvious that the former

Confederacy would only truly uphold the Thirteenth Amendment. (The Reconstruction Era is the name given to the period following the Civil War, lasting from 1865 to 1876, during which the defeated Southern states were admitted back into the Union.)

Though many white Southerners had not owned slaves, they refused to treat former blacks as equals. In many places, African Americans outnumbered whites in the South. The idea of the black community joining together to gain political power caused a lot of fear among whites.

Different methods, some legal and some not, were used to keep blacks separate from whites and too frightened to challenge the way things were. So-called **"Jim Crow laws"** made segregation the law of the land in the South. Under **segregation**, whites and blacks were forbidden to mix with each other in public places. **Mob** action and terrorist activity, by groups such as the Ku Klux Klan, were used to intimidate African Americans, especially those who showed any **defiance**. The primary method of causing such terror was lynching.

SEPARATE BUT EQUAL

The South's legal system left blacks without justice or protection. Violent crimes by whites against blacks almost always went unpunished. In 1896, in the case known as *Plessy v. Ferguson*, the **U.S. Supreme Court** ruled that segregation was not against the Constitution. The Court held that the races could be legally separated so long as both received equal services and facilities. The ruling became known as the "separate but equal" doctrine. In the years ahead, southern whites continuously relied on it to justify segregation. Laws in every Southern state made certain that schools, hospitals, churches, playgrounds, graveyards, swimming pools, restaurants, and drinking fountains remained segregated.

The facilities blacks and whites used were separate, but they were rarely equal. From schools to hospitals, black (or "colored" in the language of the time) facilities were usually inferior.

A black man drinks from a "colored" water cooler in Alabama in the 1930s.

THE GREAT MIGRATION

Hoping for a change, between 1910 and 1930, over a million blacks headed north. (Between 1940 and 1970, four million more Southern blacks went north.) However, many Northern whites also felt superior to African Americans. They did not want blacks living in their neighborhoods or attending school with their children. For the most part, African Americans lived in poor housing in the worst sections of Northern cities. These rundown, high crime areas became known as ghettos. Although segregation was not the law in the North, in effect, blacks and whites often lived segregated lives. A famous African-American author, Claude Brown, who wrote about the children of the great migration, wrote that blacks who had moved to the North from the South often ended up feeling like they had gone "from the frying pan into the fire."

AFRICAN AMERICANS IN THE MILITARY

More than 350,000 African Americans served the United States in the armed forces during World War I (1914–1918). More than one million African Americans served in World War II (1939–1945). Despite this undeniable proof of their patriotism, these veterans returned home to segregation and other forms of **discrimination**. But in the aftermath of World War II, they and their friends and loved ones were less willing to accept such treatment.

This Coca-Cola machine marked "White Customers Only!" gives some indication of how deeply segregated southern society was in the first decades of the 20th century.

Groups and individuals challenged the system. One of the first and most important challenges came from the National Association for the Advancement of Colored People (NAACP), a civil rights organization founded in 1909. For decades, the NAACP had used the legal system to challenge discrimination. By the 1950s, it was focusing on segregation in public schools.

BROWN V. THE BOARD OF EDUCATION

1954 brought a stunning victory for the NAACP, for African Americans, and for all Americans interested in freedom and equality. That year, the U.S. Supreme Court ruled in the case of *Brown v. The Board of Education*. The NAACP had sued the Board of Education in Topeka, Kansas, after it refused to allow an African-American girl to attend an all-white public school.

The legal strategy was devised by a group of African-American lawyers from the NAACP Legal Defense and Education Fund. The group's leader was a brilliant young attorney from Maryland named Thurgood Marshall. Marshall argued that segregated schools harmed African-American students by making them feel that they were not as good as whites. Marshall stressed that this affected their ability to learn. Marshall's most important point was that there could never be any such thing as "separate but equal." Separation automatically meant unequal.

Marshall's arguments convinced the Supreme Court. In a unanimous decision on May 17, 1954, the Court stated, "We conclude that in the field of public education, the doctrine of 'separate but equal' has no place. Separate educational facilities are inherently unequal."

The *Brown* ruling made segregation illegal in public schools nationwide. Yet it was just another first step in the African-American fight for equality. Unfortunately, the Court had not required public schools to desegregate by a specific date, nor directed them as to how they should achieve **desegregation**. Also, the ruling applied only to public schools, although it was easy to foresee that it might soon be extended to other public facilities.

HE MADE A DIFFERENCE

As chief counsel for the NAACP Legal Defense and Education Fund, Thurgood Marshall challenged segregation in both schools and housing. In 1967, he became the first African American appointed to the U.S. Supreme Court, the nation's highest court.

Many whites resisted the ruling. It sparked a huge backlash in parts of the South. Many southerners referred to the date of the ruling as "Black Monday." White violence against blacks increased. A new kind of hate group, known as the White Citizens' Council (WCC), was formed, first in Greenwood, Mississippi, and then throughout the South. The WCC focused on holding back blacks economically. "The purpose," one WCC member said, "is to make it difficult, if not impossible, for any Negro who advocates desegregation to find a job, get credit, or renew a mortgage."

THE DEATH OF EMMETT TILL

In August 1955, Emmett Till, an outgoing, black youth from the northern city of Chicago, Illinois, was visiting relatives in Money, a small town in the Mississippi Delta. One evening, Emmett allegedly whistled at a young white woman who worked in a general store.

A few nights later, Emmett was kidnapped at gunpoint from the home of his great-uncle, Moses Wright, and brutally beaten, shot, and then dumped into a river with a cotton gin fan tied around his neck with barbed wire. The murderers were the husband of the woman in the store and her brother-in-law. When Till was pulled from the

This was the last photograph taken of 14-year-old Emmett Till when he was alive. "If there was a group there, Emmett was in front," a friend remembered. "And he was the lively one. He was the one that everybody kind of looked to. Natural born leader."

Mamie Till breaks down at the sight of the coffin that carried the mutilated body of her murdered son from Mississippi back home to Chicago. At his wake, Mamie insisted that Emmett's body be displayed in an open coffin, without being touched up by the undertaker. "Let the people see what I've seen," she told the funeral director. Later, she said of that decision, "I think everybody needed to know what had happened to Emmett Till."

THE WHOLE TRUTH

When Moses Wright took the witness stand at the trial, it was the first time in Mississippi that a black man had dared to testify against whites. It meant risking his life. His courage empowered another black witness to step forward as well. Both men had to be smuggled out of Mississippi after the trial, never to return.

river, he could only be identified by the initialed, gold ring on his hand. It once belonged to his father, who died while serving in the military during World War II.

Till's body was taken back for burial to Chicago, where his mother, Mamie, allowed it to be viewed. She felt that the whole world should see. An estimated 50,000 African Americans attended his funeral services in Chicago. As they passed the open casket, many fainted, yelled out in anger, or collapsed into tears. By the time of the trial of his murderers, back in the Mississippi Delta, the story was front-page news around the world.

J.W. Milam (left) and Roy Bryant (right) sit with their mother in the Sumner, Mississippi, courthouse where they were tried for the murder of Emmett Till. In the confession he gave to *Look* magazine, Milam said that he needed to "make an example" of Till, because "as long as I can live and do something about it, niggers are going to stay in their place. [They] ain't gonna vote where I live . . . They ain't gonna go to school with my kids."

The all-white jury found the defendants not guilty. Not long after the trial, the defendants confessed—for a payment of $4,000—to their crimes to a national news magazine.

Till's murder and the verdict inspired many Americans, black and white, into action for **civil rights**. His mother, Mamie Till, remained an activist until her death in 2003. Speaking at a rally shortly after her son's death, she said, "Two months ago I had a nice apartment in Chicago. I had a good job. I had a son. When something happened to [blacks] in the South I said, 'That's their business, not mine.' Now I know how wrong I was. The murder of my son has shown me that what happens to any of us, anywhere in the world, had better be the business of us all."

THE MOTHER OF THE CIVIL RIGHTS MOVEMENT

The incident often credited as the official start of the civil rights movement took place on December 1, 1955, in Montgomery, Alabama. Rosa Parks, a black **seamstress**, refused to give up her seat on a Montgomery bus. According to Montgomery law, African-American passengers were required to move to the back of the bus if a white person wanted their seat.

This day, however, Parks refused to move. The white bus driver called the police, and Parks was arrested.

THE MONTGOMERY BUS BOYCOTT

Black leaders in Montgomery decided to stage a city-wide bus **boycott** on the day of Rosa Park's trial, December 5, 1955. The organizers quickly produced 3,500 flyers to alert

MYTH AND REALITY

For years, many people thought Rosa Parks refused to give up her seat on the bus because her feet were tired. This is untrue. In fact, she had discussed a protest of this kind with local civil rights leaders. As Parks later wrote, "My feet were not tired, but I was tired—tired of unfair treatment."

17

Rosa Parks recreates for a photographer her refusal to give up her seat on a Montgomery city bus in 1955. Many people regard Parks' courageous act as the true starting point of the modern civil rights movement.

the community. **Car pools** were organized. African Americans who owned taxi companies agreed to drive African-American passengers that day for the price of bus fare.

The boycott was a spectacularly successful demonstration of African-American unity. A reporter from the *Atlanta Journal* described the scene like this: "Negroes were on almost every street corner in the downtown area, silent, waiting for rides or moving about to keep warm, but few got on buses . . . No one spoke to white people. They exchanged little talk among themselves. It was an almost solemn event."

It was then decided to continue the boycott. The Montgomery Improvement Association (MIA) was quickly organized to lead the protest. Dr. Martin Luther King, Jr., the new minister at the Dexter Avenue Baptist Church, was picked to head the MIA.

King was an outstanding speaker who believed in the power of **nonviolent resistance**. He taught his followers to return hate with Christian love. If taunted, the boycotters were to ignore the taunts. If attacked, they were not to fight back. They had to be willing to accept being arrested and jailed for their actions. King said, "If we protest courageously, and yet with dignity and Christian love, when the history books are written in the future, someone will have to say, 'There lived a race of people, of black people, of people who had the moral courage to stand up for their rights.'"

During the boycott Dr. King and other MIA leaders met with city commissioners and bus company representatives. Over 150 volunteers drove people to work. Some black churches bought station wagons for that purpose as well. Thousands of people walked long distances. They felt it was a small price to pay for equality. When an elderly black woman was asked if she was weary from such walking, she replied, "My feet are tired, but my soul is at rest."

The white community responded violently. On January 30, 1956, Dr. King's home was bombed while he was at a church meeting. His wife and seven-week-old child escaped injury. At other times, he and other leaders were threatened, humiliated, and even arrested. The boycott continued. Finally, in November 1956, the U.S. Supreme Court ruled that segregation on city buses was **unconstitutional**. On December 21, 1956, the Montgomery bus boycott officially ended. Whites could no longer legally keep African Americans at the back of the bus.

Following the boycott, King and other civil rights leaders founded the Southern Christian Leadership Conference (SCLC). They looked for other ways to practice nonviolent resistance to segregation. Soon important changes began to occur.

THE LITTLE ROCK NINE

Young people performed some of the most heroic acts of the civil rights movement. These brave individuals made enormous sacrifices. This was the case in 1957 in Little Rock, Arkansas.

A U.S. Army infantryman stands guard outside Central High School, in Little Rock, Arkansas, in early September 1957.

Elizabeth Eckford is taunted by whites as she attempts to make her way to Central High School in September 1957.

Little Rock had been slow to **integrate** its schools. When its all-white Central High School was forced to accept nine African-American students in September 1957, everyone expected trouble. Arkansas governor Orval E. Faubus had the Arkansas National Guard surround the building to keep out the black students.

Elizabeth Eckford, one of the nine African-American students, attempted to enter the school alone. White teenagers casually walked past the Arkansas guardsmen. When Eckford

A soldier helps a young African-American man with his bicycle during the disturbances that marked the desegregation of Central High School in Little Rock, Arkansas.

reached the door, however, the guardsmen glared at her and raised their rifles.

Turned away from the entrance, Eckford now faced an angry white mob that had gathered in front of the school. She tried to make it through the crowd to the bus stop. Furious whites ripped her clothes and clawed at her skin. Someone in the crowd threatened to drag her over to a tree and lynch her. Fortunately two other whites stepped forward and led her to safety.

Finally, President Dwight D. Eisenhower sent in U.S. troops to protect the black students. Even so, it was never easy for the African Americans at Central High. During the year they were

* * * *

spat on, insulted, kicked, and hit. But the "Little Rock Nine," as they came to be called, accomplished an important task. They helped pave the way for school integration throughout the South.

THE SIT-INS

There were other areas of segregation still to be challenged. African Americans could shop at certain stores, such as Woolworth's (a five-and-dime store), but they could not be served or eat at the lunch counter. On February 1, 1960, four African-American students from North Carolina's A&T College sat down at the lunch counter in the Woolworth's in Greensboro, North Carolina. When they were not served, they stayed in their seats until the store closed. This form of protest is known as a **sit-in**.

Demonstrators "sit in" at a lunch counter in Woolworth's department store in Greensboro, North Carolina, in 1960. These young protestors, and hundreds more like them, were trained in nonviolence and refused to retaliate even when threatened and attacked by white citizens and arrested and abused by police.

The following day twenty-nine more African-American students joined them. None were served, but the protestors were not discouraged. Sixty-three students came on the third day of the sit-in.

Before long, the Student Nonviolent Coordinating Committee (SNCC; usually pronounced as "snick") was formed to help organize and direct such protests. Like the SCLC, SNCC believed in the idea of nonviolence. SNCC and other groups held sit-ins at segregated lunch counters in other cities and states. Soon there were fifty-four sit-ins in five cities in nine Southern states.

Victory did not come easily. In some places, stores closed their lunch counters. In others, they removed the chairs or stools. Then, the young protestors stood. They took shifts doing so until closing time. During many sit-ins, the protestors faced taunts and violence. Nevertheless, they responded nonviolently.

In time, the sit-ins worked. The Woolworth's in Greensboro desegregated its lunch counter by July 1960. Sit-ins also led to changes at segregated libraries, museums, and parks.

FREEDOM RIDERS

By 1961, **interstate transportation** should have been completely integrated. A civil rights group known as the Congress of Racial Equality (CORE) had successfully argued this issue before the U.S. Supreme Court as early as 1946. Yet the desegregation ruling had been ignored throughout the South.

Freedom riders depart Washington, D.C., in 1961 on the first leg of their journey to desegregate interstate travel in the South. The hopefulness and good cheer visible in the young people here would be met by hatred and violence as the buses traveled further south.

In the summer of 1961, a group of mostly young blacks and whites planned to ride together by bus through the South from Washington, D.C., to New Orleans, Louisiana, which was about a two-week trip. They planned to sit together on the bus in integrated groups. The African Americans planned to use the "whites-only" waiting rooms

The freedom riders' bus burst into flames outside Anniston, Alabama, after being firebombed by white supremacists. Even the presence of undercover FBI agents among the freedom riders did not protect them from violence.

in the bus terminals as well. The demonstrators called the protest a "freedom ride."

James Farmer, the head of CORE, recalled what the freedom riders expected: "We were told that the racists, the segregationists, would go to any extent to hold the line on segregation in interstate travel. So when we began the ride, I think all of us were prepared for as much violence as could be thrown at us. We were prepared for the possibility of death." Some freedom riders prepared their wills before boarding the bus. Many also wrote letters to their families that were to be delivered if they didn't return.

When a bus stopped in Anniston, Alabama, a mob of about 200 whites stoned the bus and slashed its tires. When the bus left, the mob followed in cars. When the tires went flat, forcing the bus to the side of the road, a firebomb was thrown inside. As the freedom riders poured out from the flames and the smoke, they were attacked with baseball bats, rocks, pipes, and bottles.

Another group of freedom riders was attacked in Birmingham, Alabama. There they were beaten with sticks and clubs or thrown to the ground and kicked when they got off the bus. One freedom rider was left paralyzed. The mob violence continued when a third bus of freedom riders reached Montgomery, Alabama. Many freedom riders had to be hospitalized. When Martin Luther King, Jr., flew to Montgomery to lead a rally of support, the church where the rally was held was surrounded and menaced by an armed white mob. The National Guard had to be sent in to protect the protestors.

The freedom rides and **demonstrations** of support continued all summer. Many demonstrators were beaten; more than 350 were arrested for "disturbing the peace" and held in jail all summer. Some of the riders were even imprisoned on death row in Mississippi's notorious Parchman prison farm. The riders never reached New Orleans. Yet their nonviolent courage earned them victory anyway. In September 1961, at the direction of Robert Kennedy, the attorney general of the United States, the Interstate Commerce Commission issued an order outlawing segregation in interstate bus travel.

This is what remained of the Sixteenth Street Baptist Church in Birmingham after the bombing in 1963. During the civil rights movement, white bombings of one black neighborhood in Birmingham were so frequent that the neighborhood became known as "Dynamite Hill."

* * * *

THE CHILDREN'S CRUSADE

By 1963, King and the SCLC were focused on Birmingham as the site of their next protest. Alabama's largest city, Birmingham was often described as the most segregated city in the United States. The particular target was Birmingham's department stores, where blacks were encouraged to shop (and spend their money) but were seldom hired.

The demonstrations, in the form of nonviolent marches downtown, began in early April 1963. The first protests were met with arrests and a court order forbidding further activity of the kind. When the protests continued, the police turned high-pressure fire hoses and police dogs on the demonstrators. The water knocked protestors to the ground

During the civil rights demonstrations in Birmingham in 1963, police used attack dogs against the demonstrators.

29

or pinned them up against buildings; the dogs bit their flesh while the police swung their billy clubs. Hundreds of more demonstrators were arrested.

Among those arrested was King. While confined, he wrote his famous and beautiful *Letter from a Birmingham Jail*, a powerful statement of the goals and ideals of the civil rights movement. African Americans had been waiting "more than 340 years" for their "constitutional and God-given rights," King wrote. Their patience was all used up, for they had been made to realize, King explained, that this "waiting" had "almost always meant never."

The last phase of the Birmingham protest became known as the Children's Crusade, as African-American children as

Another tactic used by the police in Birmingham against civil rights activists was to "spray" them with water from high-pressure fire hoses. The force of such spraying was strong enough to knock a person off his or her feet.

Martin Luther King, Jr., contemplates the state of American society from behind the bars of a Birmingham jail in April 1963. When asked by other members of the clergy why he was in Birmingham, King responded, in his famous *Letter from a Birmingham Jail*, "I am in Birmingham because injustice is here."

young as six marched in the protests. This made no difference to the Birmingham police, and the fire hoses and dogs were brought out again, this time against children as well as adults.

The 1963 events in Birmingham led to a new wave of civil rights protests. Nearly one thousand demonstrations were held in more than one hundred Southern cities. There were marches, sit-ins, and boycotts. Over 20,000 civil rights workers were jailed.

A new civil rights bill to guarantee equal rights for African Americans had been proposed. Civil rights leaders urged Congress to pass it. To stress their demands, a massive demonstration was planned to take place at the nation's capital. It was known as the March on Washington.

31

With the Washington Monument looming symbolically in the background, a huge crowd gathers to hear Martin Luther King, Jr., and other famous speakers and performers at the March on Washington, August 28, 1963.

(From left) Denise McNair, age 11; Carole Robertson, age 14; Addie Mae Collins, age 14; and Cynthia Wesley, age 14, were the four girls killed in the bombing by white supremacists of the Sixteenth Street Baptist Church in Birmingham, Alabama, in 1963.

On August 28, 1963, more than 250,000 people peacefully gathered in Washington, D.C. They prayed, sang, and listened to speeches. Dr. Martin Luther King, Jr., addressed the crowd. It was here that he gave the moving "I have a dream" speech for which he is perhaps most famous.

On July 2, 1964, President Lyndon B. Johnson signed the Civil Rights Act of 1964. It was hailed as the most far-reaching civil rights law of the century. The new law stopped government funding for programs that discriminated against blacks. It also protected the African-American's right to fairness in employment and to use public facilities. In addition, the Act insured the voting rights of black Americans. However, in some parts of the South, people refused to obey the law. Therefore, King organized further protests to enable more African Americans to vote.

BIRMINGHAM CHURCH BOMBING

On September 15, 1963, the Sixteenth Street Baptist Church in Birmingham was bombed. Four African-American girls, aged 11 to 14, were killed. Three men were eventually convicted for the crime. The last one, Bobby Frank Cherry, was tried and convicted in 2002. Unfortunately, it took thirty-nine years for justice to be done.

President Lyndon B. Johnson hands Martin Luther King, Jr., the pen with which he signed the Civil Rights Act of 1964 into law.

THE MISSISSIPPI FREEDOM SUMMER

Mississippi segregationists had long claimed that blacks were not interested in voting, but the truth was that most blacks were too frightened to vote. Whites selectively enforced laws such as the poll tax and literacy tests to keep blacks from voting. Blacks who insisted on exercising their right to vote were threatened with losing their jobs and even violence. Many were beaten; several were murdered. In the fall of 1963, Robert Moses, a New York teacher and SNCC activist, organized what he called the Freedom Vote.

Student volunteers from the North came to Mississippi and walked door to door in black neighborhoods, campaigning for a practice election, which was intended to familiarize blacks, many of whom had never voted, with the political process. On "election day," 93,000 Mississippi blacks practiced participating in the political process.

In the summer of 1964, with the presidential election quickly approaching, it was time for the real thing. Again, Robert Moses recruited workers, this time for what he called the Mississippi Freedom Summer, the primary goal of which was voter registration and the establishment of "freedom schools." The Mississippi Freedom Democratic Party (MFDP) was established to challenge the all-white Mississippi Democratic Party.

By summer's end, freedom schools were filled with black people of all ages, eager to learn lessons in subjects such as math and reading, and, for the very first time, black history and culture. Eighty thousand blacks joined the Mississippi Freedom Democratic Party.

The MFDP then tried to gain seats for its delegates at the National Democratic Convention held in Atlantic City, New Jersey. They contested the established Mississippi Democrats as not being a fair representation of the true population of Mississippi voters. Though the Mississippi Democrats

This FBI "missing" poster seeks information about the whereabouts of (from left) Andrew Goodman, James Earl Chaney, and Michael Henry Schwerner, civil rights workers who had disappeared in Mississippi during the "freedom summer" of 1964. They had been arrested by the sheriff of Neshoba County, Mississippi, who was also a member of the KKK.

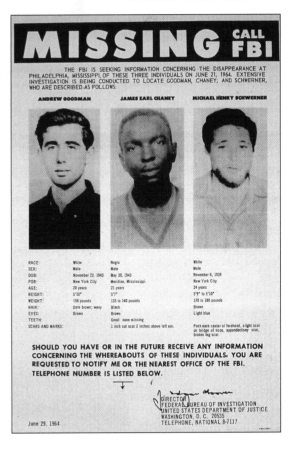

* * * *

did succeed in retaining their seats for the convention, the MFDP challenge was widely debated and publicized. It led to increased opportunities in the Democratic party for blacks and other minorities who had long been supporters but had not been fairly represented.

THE SELMA-TO-MONTGOMERY MARCH

A nighttime march for voting rights was held in Selma, Alabama, on February 18, 1965. But as the march began,

THE FREEDOM SUMMER MURDERS

Three young men who volunteered for the Freedom Summer voter registration drive were James Earl Chaney, Michael Henry Schwerner, and Andrew Goodman. On June 24, 1964, the trio was jailed briefly in Philadelphia, Mississippi, on phony traffic charges and then released. However, they never returned from jail that night. Twenty-two Klansmen stopped their car on the road and killed them. Their shot and beaten bodies were found forty-four days later buried in a dam.

The car that carried Schwerner, Chaney, and Goodman is pulled from the river in which it was dumped by their murderers. Their families wanted the three men to be buried together in the churchyard of Mt. Zion Baptist Church in Philadelphia, Mississippi, but at the time it was against the law in Mississippi for blacks and whites to be buried together.

36

Marchers link arms on the road to Montgomery, the state capital of Alabama, from Selma in late March 1965. The goal we seek, Martin Luther King, Jr., told the marchers once they had reached Montgomery, "is a society at peace with itself, a society that can live with its conscience."

the street lights suddenly went out. Seconds later the demonstrators were attacked by police, state troopers, and angry whites. One eighty-two-year-old man, who'd been beaten, was bleeding badly. His twenty-six-year-old grandson, Jimmy Lee Jackson, helped him get to a nearby café, where several state troopers followed them in. A trooper hit Jackson's mother, who had participated in the march. When Jimmy Lee struck back to help his mother, the trooper hit him in the face with a stick. Another took out his gun and

An African American fills out a ballot during a Democratic primary election in Wilcox County, Alabama, in 1966.

Unable to take part themselves, women applaud the Selma-to-Montgomery marchers from their front porch. "In a real sense this afternoon," King told the marchers in Montgomery on March 25, 1965, "we can say that our feet are tired, but our souls are rested."

shot the young man in the stomach. Jimmy Lee Jackson died in the hospital a week later.

A memorial march for Jackson was held on March 7, but problems arose. This time, the marchers intended to walk from Selma to Montgomery, the state capital and the cradle of the civil rights movement, where Rosa Parks had made her lonely gesture. Early that Sunday morning, about 600 marchers were confronted by 200 state troopers while crossing the Edmund Pettus Bridge in Selma. The troopers, who were mounted on horses, used night sticks, tear gas, and bull whips on the pro-testors. Some marchers were trampled by the horses.

Once again, the public in much of the United States was outraged by the incident. At that point, Congress had to do something more to help. The assistance came in the form of the Voting Rights Act of 1965, which provided greater

The heavyweight boxing champion of the world, Muhammad Ali, as he refuses to be inducted into the armed services to fight in the Vietnam War. "I got no quarrel with them Vietcong," said Ali about refusing to be drafted into the army. "No Vietcong ever called me 'nigger.'"

protection for blacks' right to vote. This was achieved by providing the federal government with the legal authority to intervene where these rights were challenged, even in state elections.

Before long, many African Americans were voting for the first time. Numerous African-American officials were elected to office. Conditions for blacks began to really change. In the years that followed, they made tremendous strides in all walks of life.

With the passage of the Voting Rights Act, the civil rights movement entered a new phase. Many younger blacks were impatient with the rate of progress. Some scorned the goals of integration and equal rights and instead advocated "black power." Many of this new generation of activists also rejected nonviolence as a tactic, saying that it was naïve and too harmful to those who practiced it. Blacks became increasingly outspoken in their opposition to certain aspects of American society. This was symbolized most clearly by the refusal of Muhammad Ali, the heavyweight boxing champion of the world, to be inducted into the military after being drafted for service in the Vietnam War.

Until 1965, civil rights had been regarded as mostly a "southern problem." But that year, King began to point out that the North and other parts of the country had their own civil rights issues. That summer, a violent riot broke out in Watts, a mostly black community in the city of Los Angeles. Troops had to be called in to end the violence. For the next several summers, similar rioting broke out in the black sections of other major northern cities, most violently in Newark and Detroit.

The riots showed clearly that black northerners were no more satisfied with their place in American society than were black southerners. Combined with the calls for black power, they also frightened many whites, even among those who had supported civil rights goals. White support for civil rights began to decline at this point.

Martin Luther King, Jr., (right) takes part in helping clean up a low-income neighborhood in the northern city of Chicago, Illinois, in 1966.

Perhaps the worst of what came to be known as the "long, hot summers" was the summer of 1968. On April 4, 1968, Dr. Martin Luther King, Jr., was in Memphis, Tennessee, to lead local sanitation workers in a protest for better wages and working conditions. While standing on the balcony of the Lorraine Motel, he was shot and killed by a white supremacist and lifelong criminal, James Earl Ray. King was just 39 years old. His death prompted riots across the country. Even the streets of the nation's capital, Washington, D.C., erupted in flame.

King's aide Andrew Young (center, right) walks in front of the mule-drawn casket bearing the dead civil right's leader's body at King's funeral in Atlanta, Georgia, in April 1968.

A solitary protestor (below) carries the American flag while walking from Selma to Montgomery, Alabama, as part of the huge march between those two cities held as a demonstration for African-American voting rights in 1965.

In his *Letter from a Birmingham Jail,* King had answered those who asked why African Americans could not be more patient. Why sit-ins? Why marches? Many whites argued that, given time, race relations would eventually "work themselves out." In response, King wrote:

Perhaps it is easy for those who have never felt the stinging darts of segregation to say, "Wait." But when you have seen vicious mobs lynch your mothers and fathers at will and drown your sisters and brothers at whim; when you have seen hate-filled policemen curse, kick and even kill your black brothers and sisters . . . when you are harried by day and haunted by night by the fact that you are [black], never quite knowing what to expect next . . . then you will understand why we find it difficult to wait.

Glossary

ancestors—family members who lived long ago

boycott—to refuse to do something as a form of protest

car pools—sharing rides or having more than one person ride in a car

challenges—things that takes a good deal of effort to do

civil rights—the rights that everyone in a society is entitled to, which insure freedom and equal treatment under the law

defiance—refusing to obey

demonstrations—form of protest

desegregation—ending the practice of separating people of different races in public places

discrimination—denying a person something solely because of a characteristic such as race or sex

integrate—make public places open to people of all races

interstate transportation—buses and trains that travel
through different states

Jim Crow laws—laws that were passed in the South to keep
the races separate

mob—an unruly group of angry people

nonviolent resistance—a tactic through which protesters
do not strike back when attacked

seamstress—a woman who sews clothes

segregation—the separation of people of different races

sit-in—a form of protest in which people remain seated to
make a point

unconstitutional—not in keeping with the U.S. Constitution

U.S. Supreme Court—the highest court in the nation.
This court determines whether laws are in keeping
with the Constitution.

Timeline: The Civil

1954	1955	1956	1957	1960	1961

1954

WHITE CUSTOMERS *Only!*

Brown v. The Board of Education. This U.S. Supreme Court decision made segregation in public schools illegal.

1955

The Montgomery bus boycott begins and lasts for nearly thirteen months.

1956

The Montgomery, Alabama, home of Dr. Martin Luther King, Jr., is bombed.

1957

The Southern Christian Leadership Conference (SCLC), a civil rights organization, is founded.

The "Little Rock Nine" integrate Central High School in Little Rock, Arkansas.

1960

Four African-American college students hold a sit-in at a lunch counter in Woolworth's in Greensboro, North Carolina. Other sit-ins are conducted in numerous Southern cities.

The Student Nonviolent Coordinating Committee (SNCC), a civil rights organization, is formed.

1961

During the summer, protesters known as Freedom Riders attempt to integrate interstate transportation services and facilities.

Rights Movement

1963

1964

1965

The Sixteenth Street Baptist Church is bombed. Four young African-American girls are killed.

The March on Washington is held in our nation's capital.

The Civil Rights Act of 1964 is enacted.

Civil rights workers James Earl Chaney, Michael Henry Schwerner and Andrew Goodman are murdered in Mississippi during a voter registration drive.

Dr. Martin Luther King, Jr., is awarded a Nobel Peace Prize for his work in civil rights.

Civil rights worker Jimmy Lee Jackson is shot during a protest in Selma, Alabama, and dies a week later.

The Voting Rights Act of 1965 is enacted.

To Find Out More

BOOKS AND JOURNALS

Andryszenski, Tricia. *The March On Washington: Gathering To Be Heard*. Brookfield, Connecticut: Millbrook Press, 1996.

Beckner, Chrisanne. *100 African Americans Who Shaped American History*. San Mateo, California: Blueword Books, 1995.

George, Charles. *Life Under the Jim Crow Laws*. San Diego, California: Lucent Books, 2000.

Hamilton, Virginia. *Many Thousands Gone: African Americans From Slavery to Freedom*. New York: Knopf, 2002.

Haskins, James. *Jesse Jackson: Civil Rights Activist*. Berkeley Heights, New Jersey: Enslow Publishers, 2000.

Haskins, Jim. *The Day Martin Luther King, Jr., Was Shot: A Photo History of the Civil Rights Movement*. New York: Scholastic, 1992.

Levine, Ellen. *If You Lived in the Time Of Martin Luther King, Jr.* New York: Scholastic, 1994.

Meltzer, Milton. *There Comes A Time: The Struggle For Civil Rights*. New York: Random House, 2002.

Rowh, Mark. *Thurgood Marshall: Civil Rights Attorney and Supreme Court Justice*. Berkeley Heights, New Jersey: Enslow Publishers, 2002.

Schraff, Ann. *Coretta Scott King: Striving For Civil Rights*. Berkeley Heights, New Jersey: Enslow Publishers, 1997.

Index

Bold numbers indicate illustrations.

Ali, Muhammad, 39, **39**

Birmingham, Alabama, **28**, 29–31

Black power, 38–39

Brown v. The Board of Education, 12–13

Chaney, James Earl, 36

Civil Rights Act of 1964, 33

Congress of Racial Equality (CORE), 24, 26

Eckford, Elizabeth, 21–22, **21**

Eisenhower, Dwight D., 22

Fifteenth Amendment, 8

Fourteenth Amendment, 8

Freedom Riders, 24–27, **25**, **26**

Goodman, Andrew, 36

Jackson, Jimmy Lee, 37–38

Jim Crow laws, 9
  see also Segregation

Johnson, Lyndon B., 33, **34**

King, Martin Luther, Jr., 18–20, 27, 29–31, **31**, 33, 40–41, **40**

Ku Klux Klan, **4**, 9

Letter from a Birmingham Jail (King), 30, 40–41

Little Rock, Arkansas, 20–23

Little Rock Nine, 20–23, **22**

March on Selma, 36–38

March on Washington, 31–32

Marshall, Thurgood, 12–13

Mississippi Freedom Democratic Party, 35–36

Mississippi Freedom Summer, 34–37

Montgomery bus boycott, 17–20

National Association for the Advancement of Colored People (NAACP), 12–13

Nonviolence, 19–20, 39

Parks, Rosa, 17-18, **18**

Plessy v. Ferguson, 9-10

Reconstruction, 8–9

Robinson, Jackie, 6

Schwerner, Michael Henry, 36

Segregation, 9–11, 17–27, 29–31

Sit-ins, 23–24, **23**

Slavery, 6–8

Southern Christian Leadership Conference (SCLC), 20, 24, 29

Student Nonviolent Coordinating Committee (SNCC), 24, 34

Thirteenth Amendment, 8–9

Till, Emmett, 14–17, **14**

U.S. Supreme Court, 9–10, 20, 24

Voting Rights Act of 1965, 38

White Citizens' Councils (WCC), 13

World War II, 3, 5, **5**, 6, 11

About the Author

Popular author **Elaine Landau** worked as a newspaper reporter, editor, and as a youth services librarian before becoming a full-time writer. She has written more than 150 nonfiction books for young people. Included in her many books for Children's Press is another Cornerstones of Freedom title, *The 2000 Presidential Election*. Ms. Landau, who has a bachelor's degree in English and journalism from New York University and a master's degree in library and information science from Pratt Institute, lives in Miami, Florida, with her husband and son.